THE ALPHABET AND MOST COMMONLY USED WORDS IN SPANISH

LANGUAGE SECOND GRADE

Children's Reading & Writing Books

BABY PROFESSOR

EDUCATION KIDS

HOLA! LET'S LEARN SPANISH!

Let's all start with the Spanish alphabet! It is called the

"Abecedario"

The Abecedario consists of 27 letters compared to the English alphabet that only has 26 letters.

Let us find out what letter was added!

ABECEDARIO

(The Alphabet)

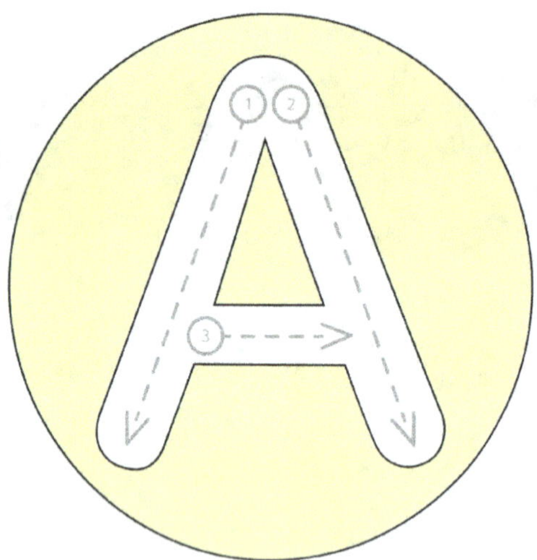

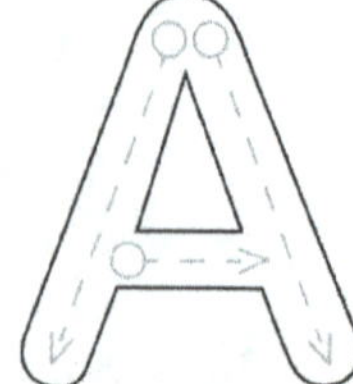

Airplane

Ant

Alligator

Airplane

Ant

Alligator

ENGLISH	SPANISH

Airplane

Airplane

Alligator

Alligator

Ant

Ant

Avión

Avión

Caimán

Caimán

Hormiga

Hormiga

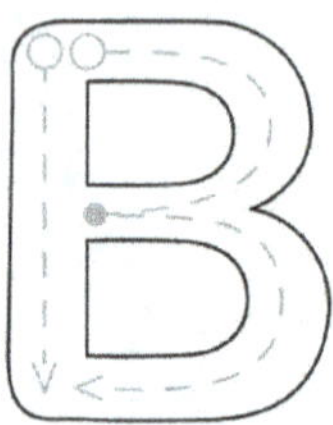

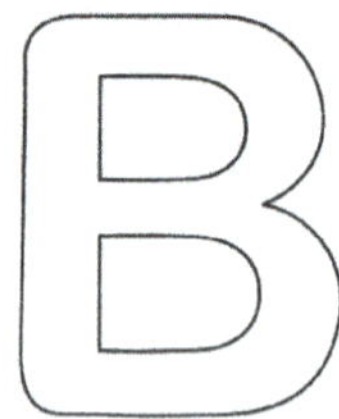

Bee

Balloon

Book

Bee

Balloon

Book

ENGLISH	SPANISH
Bee	**Abeja**
Balloon	**Libro**
Balloon	**Globo**

Sight Words

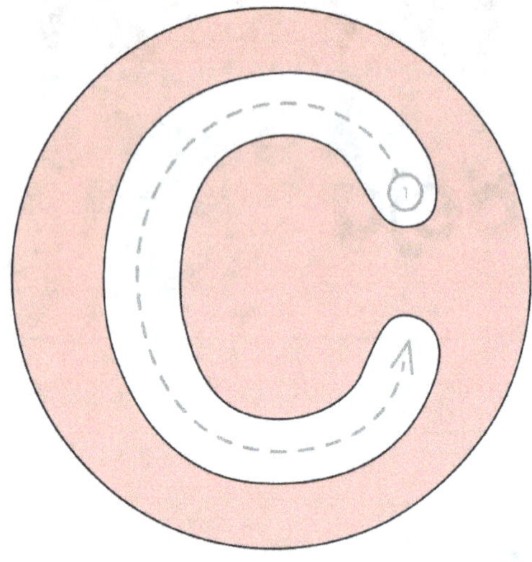

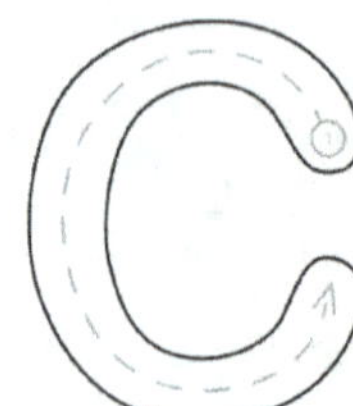

Cap

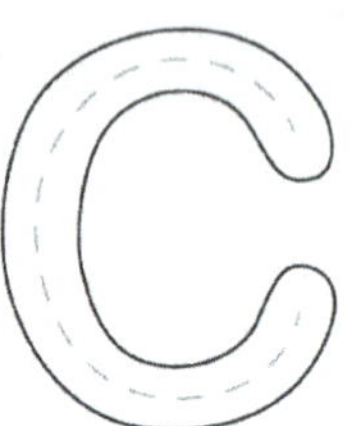

Candle

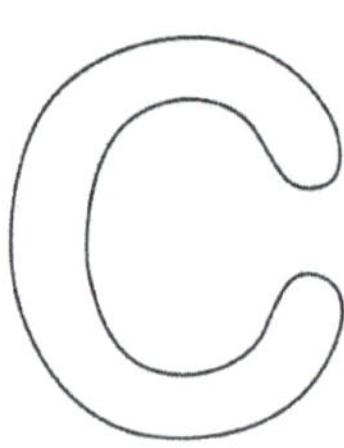

Cake

Cap

Candle

Cake

Cap

Cap

Gorra

Gorra

Cake

Cake

Pastel

Pastel

Candle

Candle

Vela

Vela

Sight Words

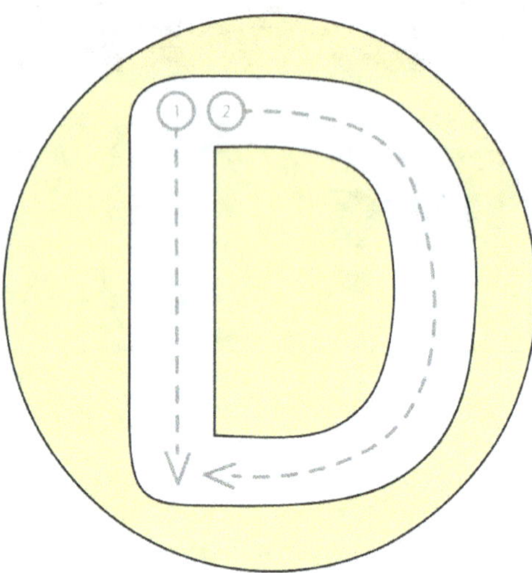

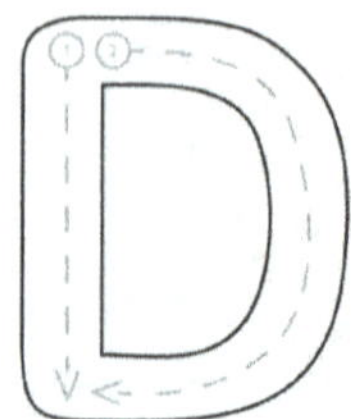

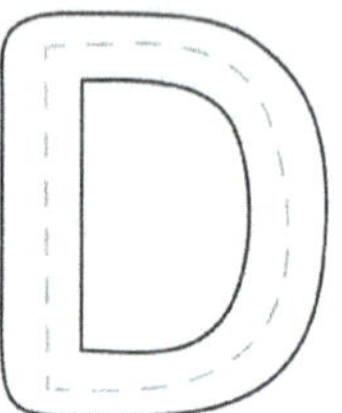

Dolphin

Drum

Duck

Dolphin

Drum

Duck

Dolphin

Dolphin

Delfín

Delfín

Duck

Duck

Pato

Pato

Drum

Drum

Tambor

Tambor

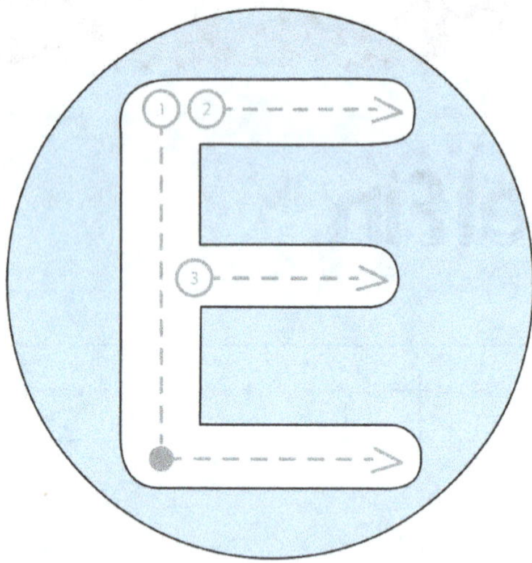

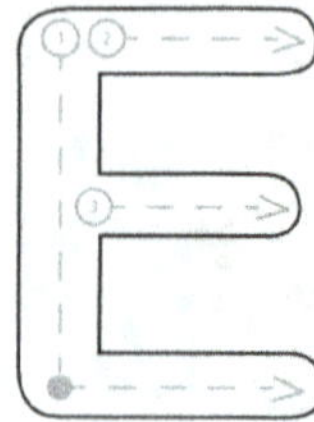

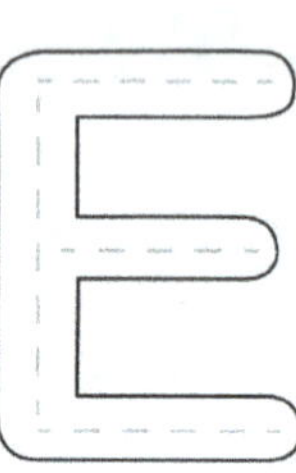

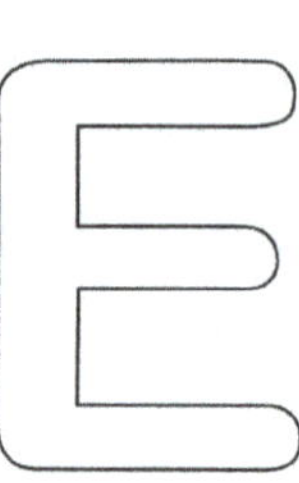

Elephant

Egg

Earth

ENGLISH	SPANISH

Elephant

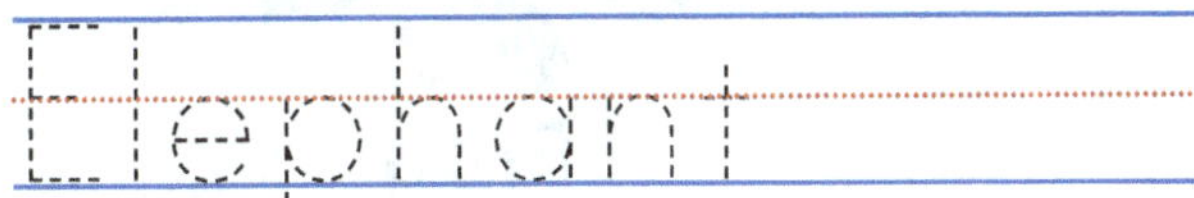

Elefante

Earth

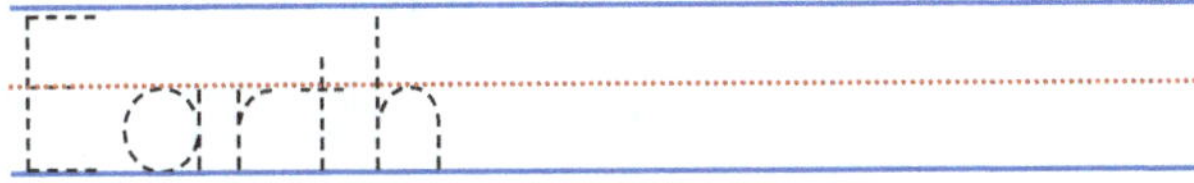

Tierra

Egg

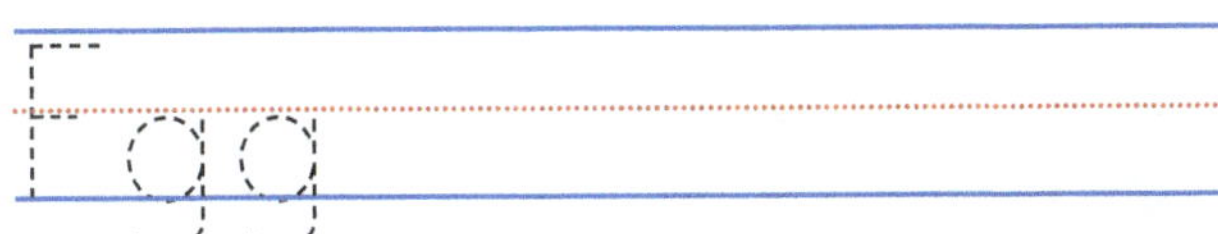

Huevo

Sight Words

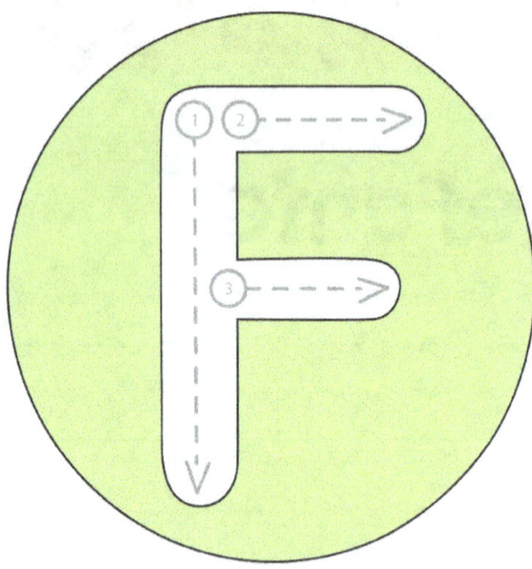

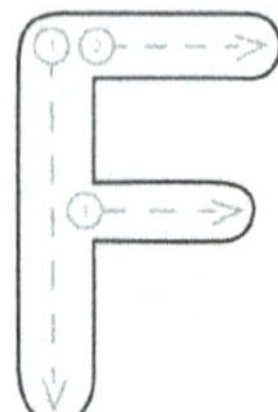

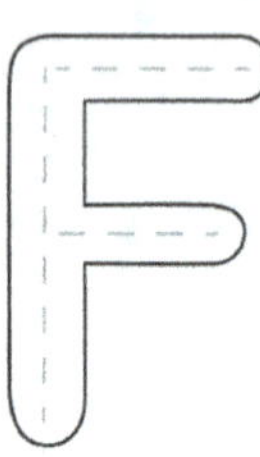

Flower

Frog

Fork

Flower

Frog

Fork

English	Spanish
Flower	Flor
Fork	Tenedor
Frog	Rana

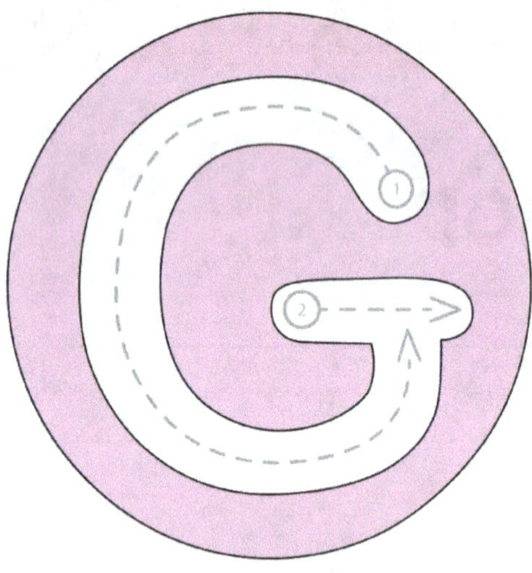

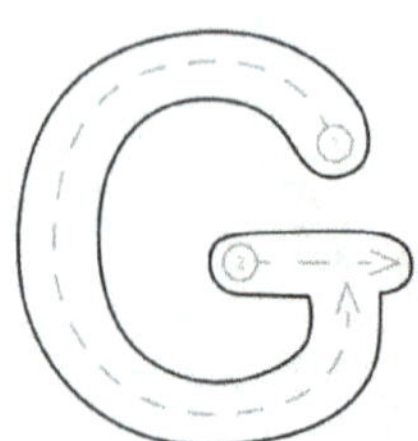
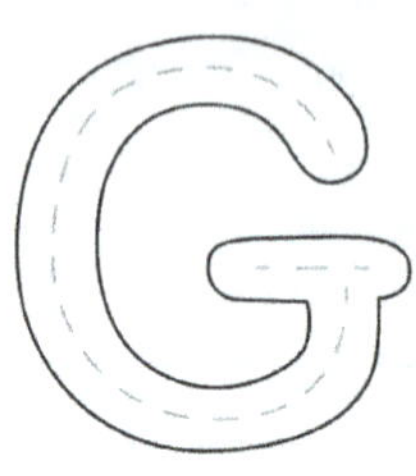

Gift

Goat

Grapes

Gift

Goat

Grapes

ENGLISH	SPANISH
Gift	**Regalo**
Gift	Regalo
Grapes	**Uva**
Grapes	Uva
Goat	**Cabra**
Goat	Cabra

Sight Words

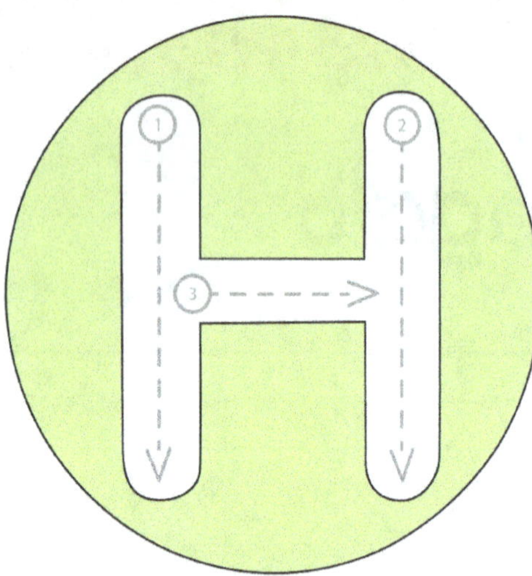

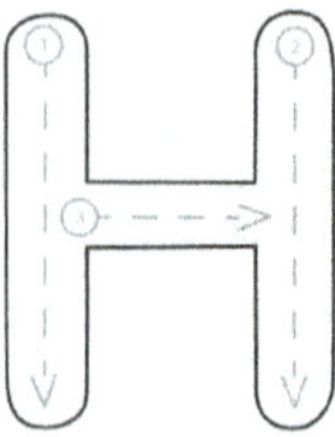
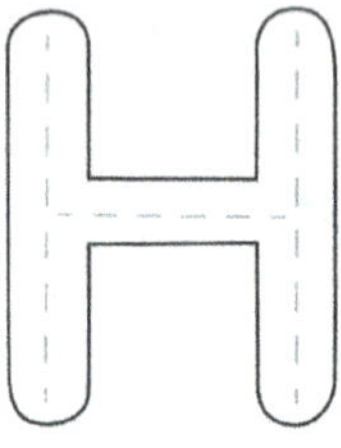
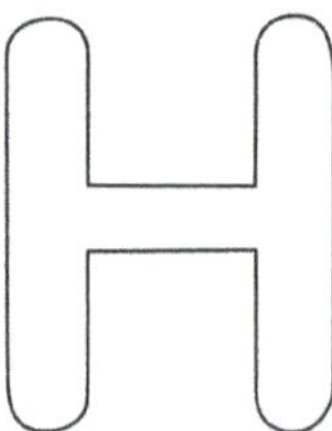

Hat

Hotdog

House

Hat

Hotdog

House

ENGLISH	SPANISH
Hat	**Sombrero**
Hat	Sombrero
House	**Casa**
House	Casa
Hotdog	**Pancho**
Hotdog	Pancho

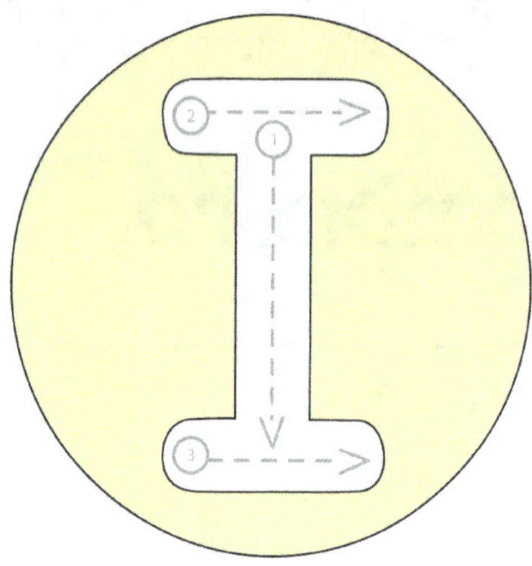

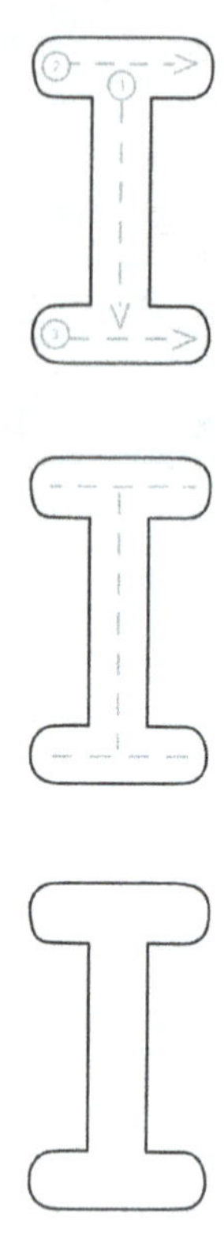

Ice cream

Island

Igloo

<table>
<tr><td></td><td></td></tr>
<tr><td>

Ice cream

Ice cream

</td><td>

Helado

Helado

</td></tr>
<tr><td>

Igloo

Igloo

</td><td>

Iglú

Iglú

</td></tr>
<tr><td>

Island

Island

</td><td>

Isla

Isla

</td></tr>
</table>

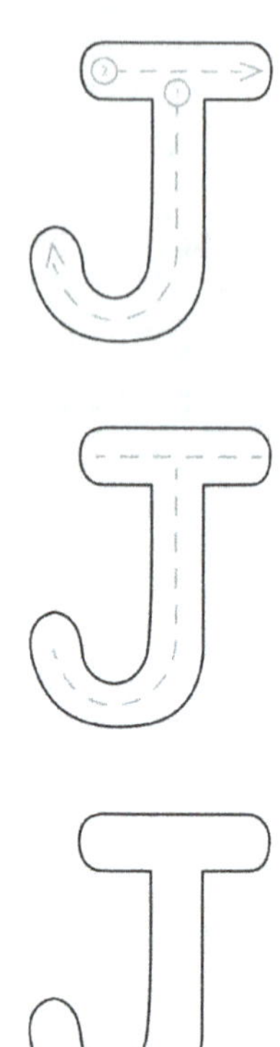

Jam

Juice

Joker

Jam

Mermelada

Joker

Bromist

Juice

Jugo

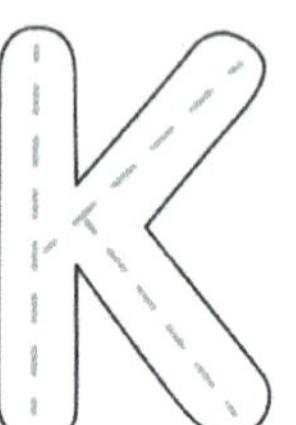

Keyboard

King

Kangaroo

Keyboard

King

Kangaroo

ENGLISH	SPANISH
Keyboard	**Helado**
Keyboard	Helado
Kangaroo	**Iglú**
Kangaroo	Iglú
King	**Isla**
King	Isla

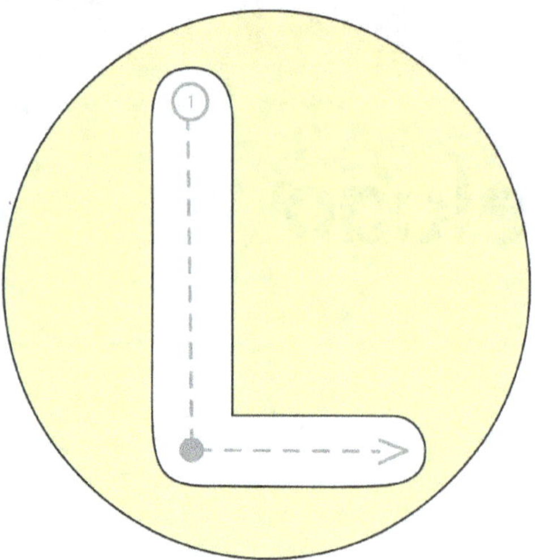

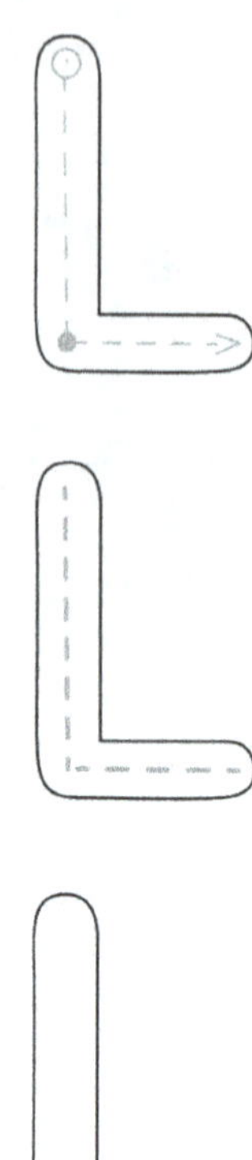

Lamp

Ladybug

Leaves

Lamp

Ladybug

Leaves

Lamp

Lamp

Leaves

Leaves

Ladybug

Ladybug

Lámpara

Lámpara

Hojas

Hojas

Mariquita

Mariquita

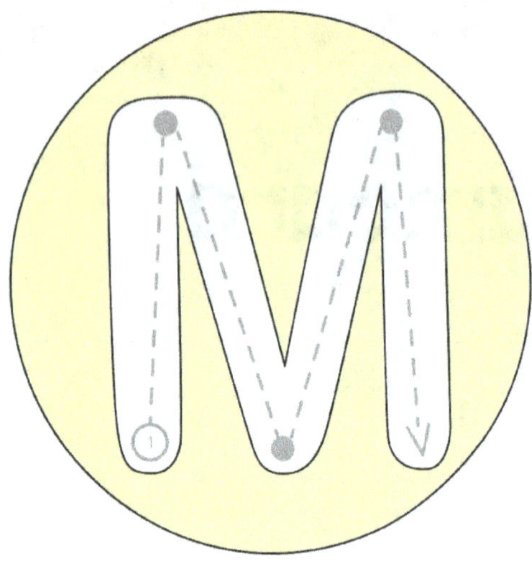

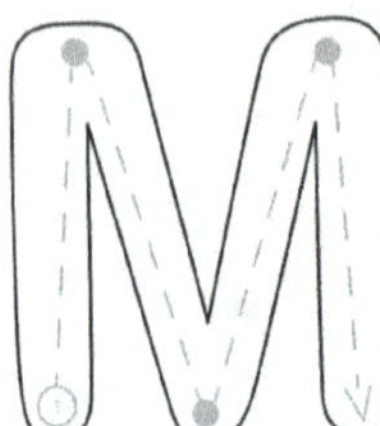

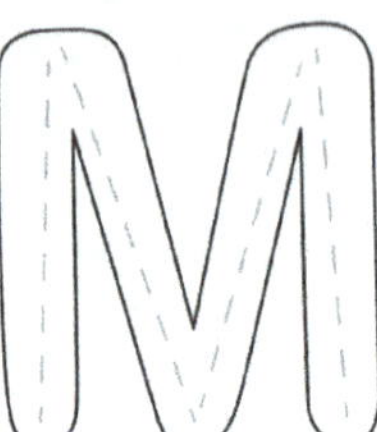

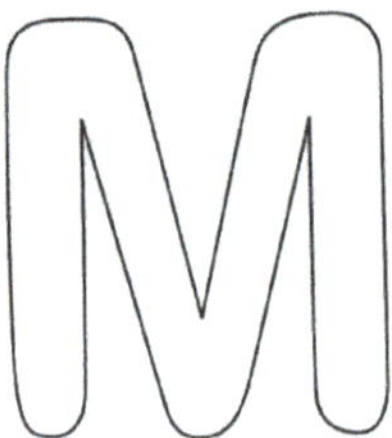

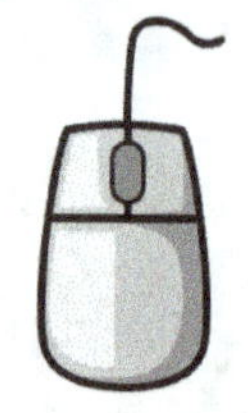
Mouse

Mushroom

Motorcycle

Mouse

Mushroom

Motorcycle

ENGLISH	SPANISH
Mouse	**Ratón**
Mouse	Ratón
Motorcycle	**Motocicleta**
Motorcycle	Motocicleta
Mushroom	**Seta**
Mushroom	Seta

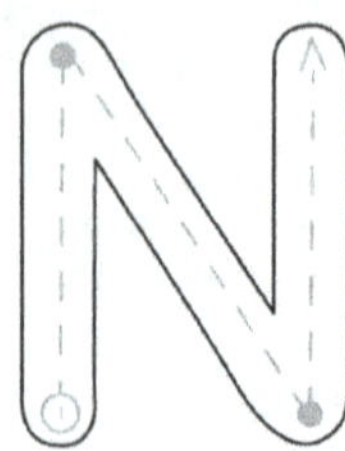

Note

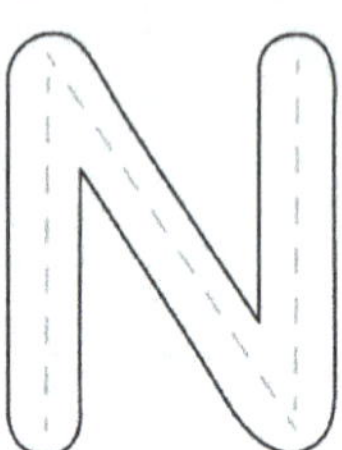

Nut

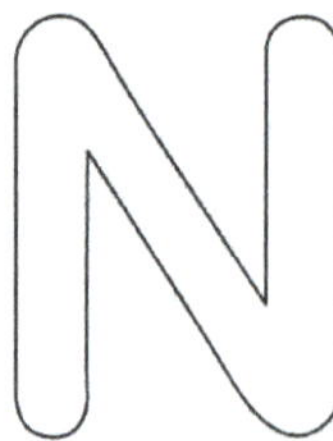

Nest

Note

Nut

Nest

<table>
<tr><td></td><td></td></tr>
</table>

ENGLISH	SPANISH
Note	**Nota**
Note	Nota
Nest	**Nido**
Nest	Nido
Nut	**Motocicleta**
Nut	Seta

Sight Words

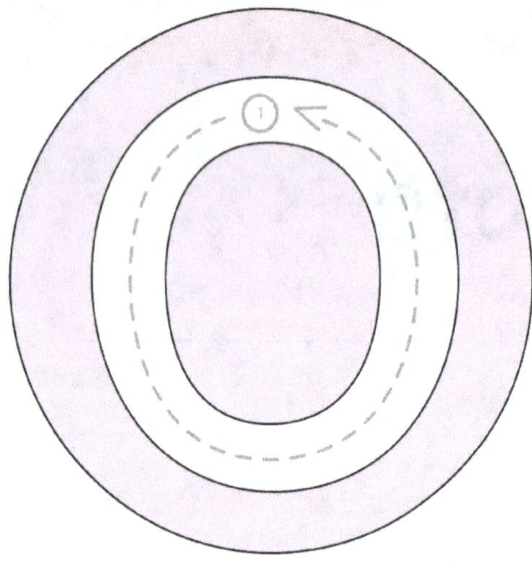

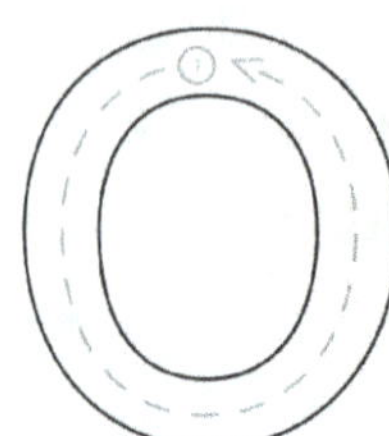

Orange

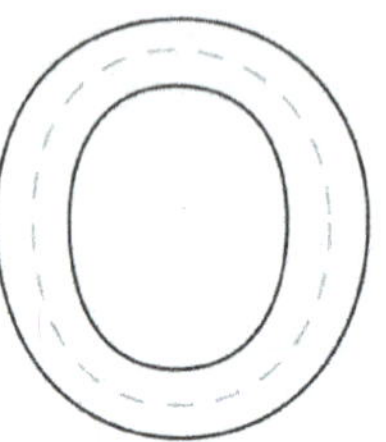

Owl

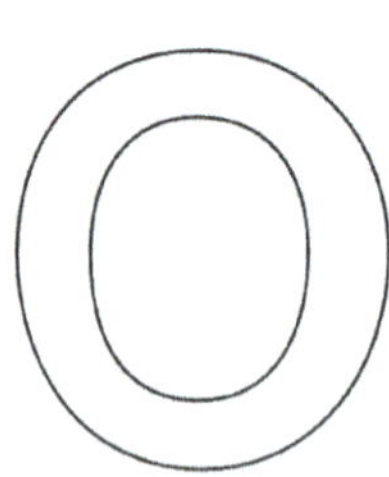

Old

Orange

Owl

Old

English	Spanish
Orange	naranja
Old	Antiguo
Owl	Búho

Pumpkin

Penguin

Pencil

ENGLISH

SPANISH

Pumpkin

Calabaza

Pumpkin

Calabaza

Pencil

Lápiz

Pencil

Lápiz

Penguin

Pingüino

Penguin

Pingüino

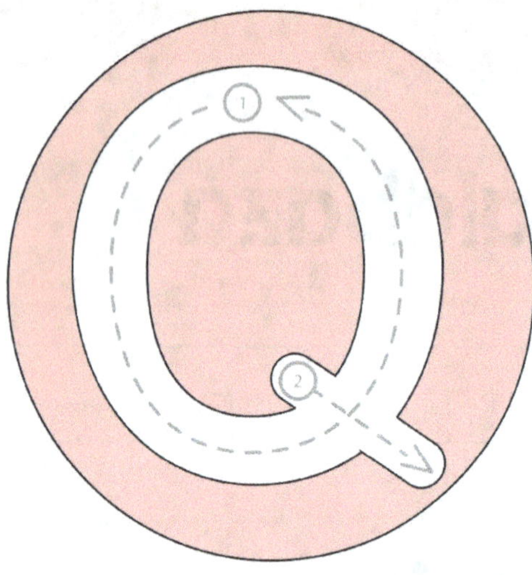

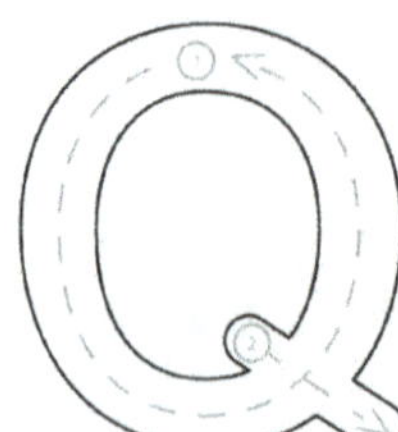

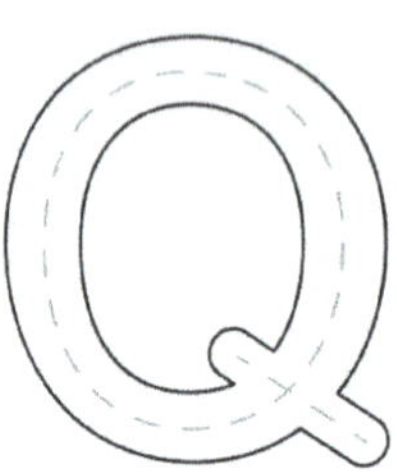

Quail

Queen

Quilt

Quail

Queen

Quilt

Quail

Quail

Codorniz

Codorniz

Quilt

Quilt

Edredón

Edredón

Queen

Queen

Reina

Reina

Sight Words

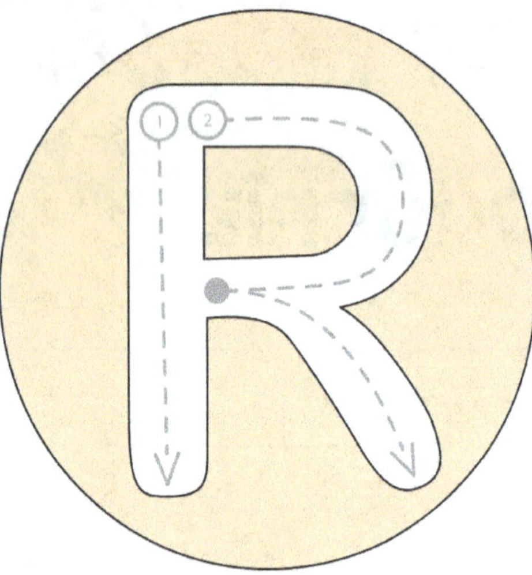

Rocket

Robot

Rabbit

Rocket

Robot

Rabbit

ENGLISH	SPANISH
Rocket	**Cohete**
Rocket	Cohete
Rabbit	**Conejo**
Rabbit	Conejo
Robot	**Robot**
Robot	Robot

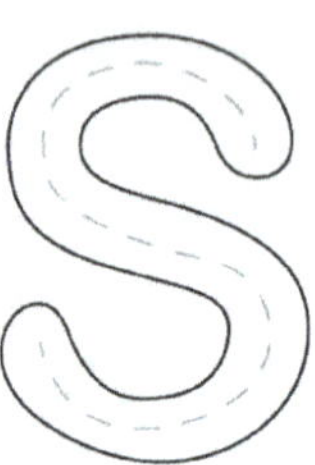

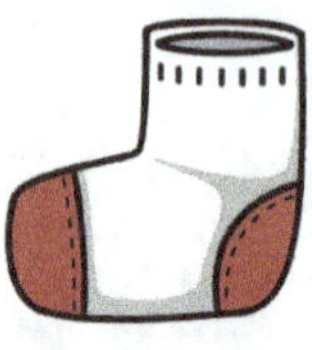

Socks

Sheep

Seal

Socks

Sheep

Seal

| | |

Socks

Socks

Seal

Seal

Sheep

Sheep

Calcetines

Calcetines

Foca

Foca

Oveja

Oveja

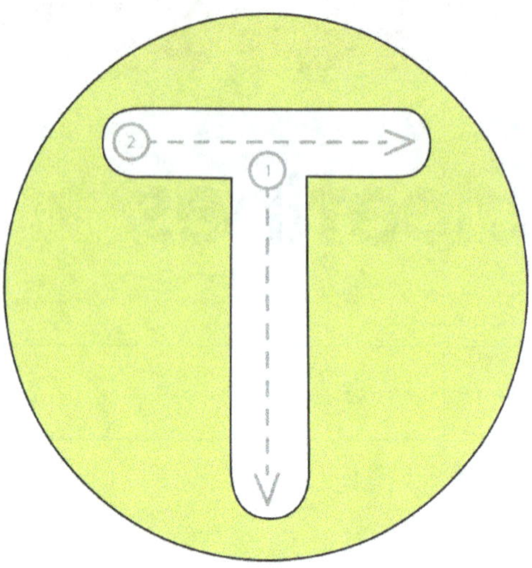

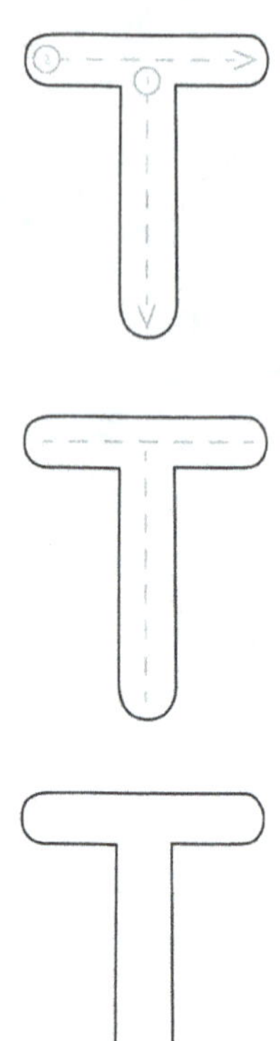

Tomato

Telephone

Turtle

Tomato   Telephone

Turtle

Tomato

Tomato

Turtle

Turtle

Telephone

Telephone

Tomate

Tomate

Tortuga

Tortuga

Teléfono

Teléfono

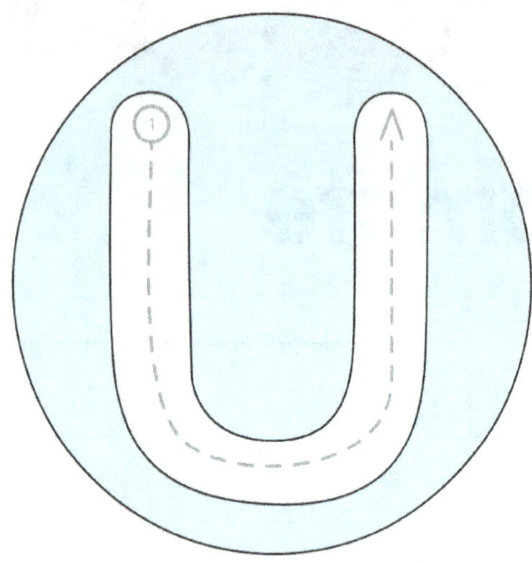

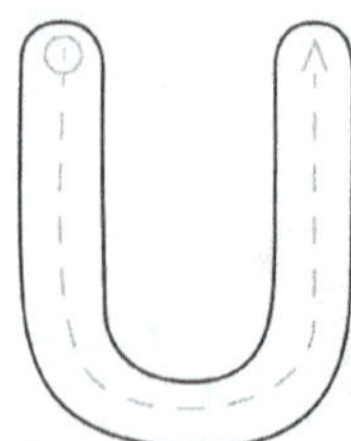

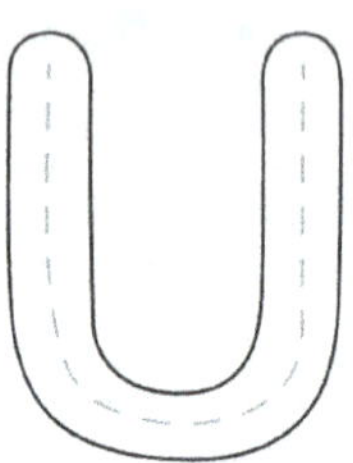

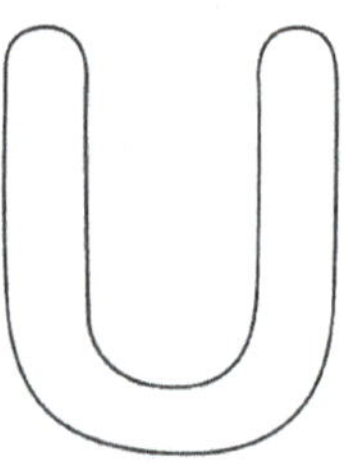

Ufo

Unicorn

Umbrella

Ufo

Unicorn

Umbrella

<table>
<tr><td>ENGLISH</td><td>SPANISH</td></tr>
<tr><td>Ufo</td><td>Ovni</td></tr>
<tr><td>Umbrella</td><td>Paraguas</td></tr>
<tr><td>Unicorn</td><td>Unicornio</td></tr>
</table>

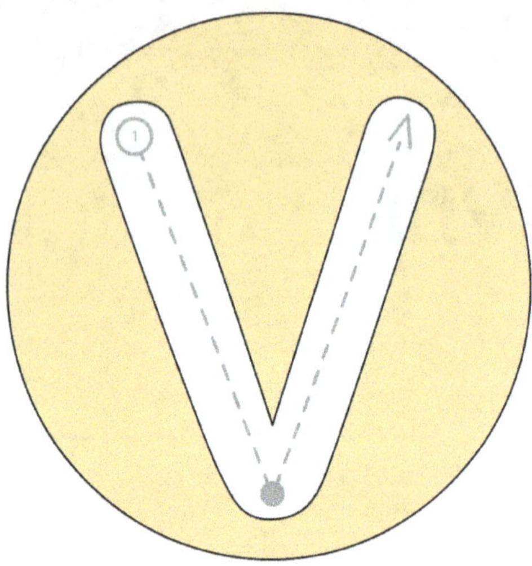

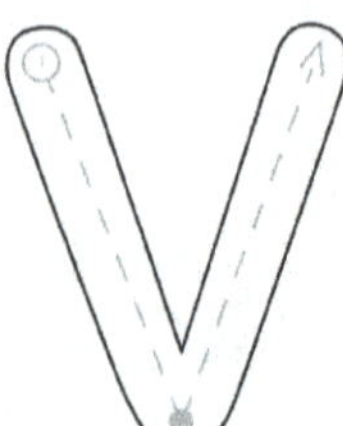

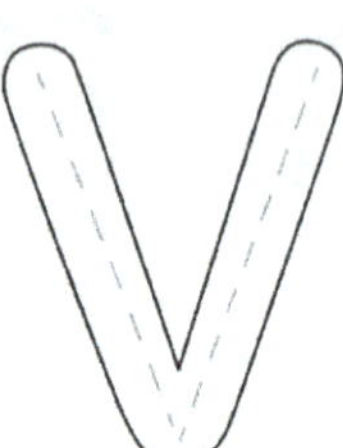

Video

Vulture

Van

ENGLISH	SPANISH
Video	Video
Van	camioneta
Vulture	Buitre

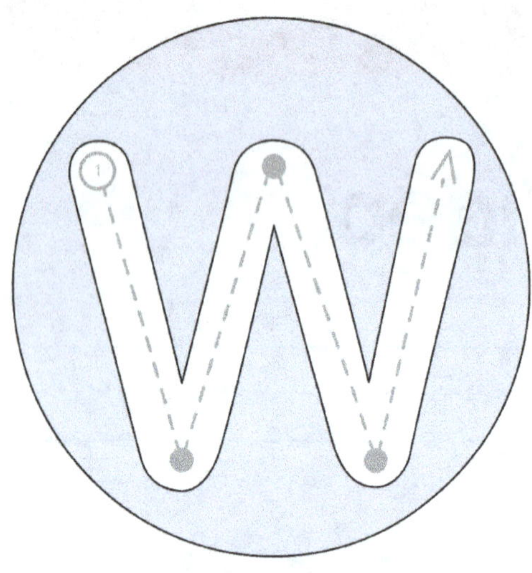

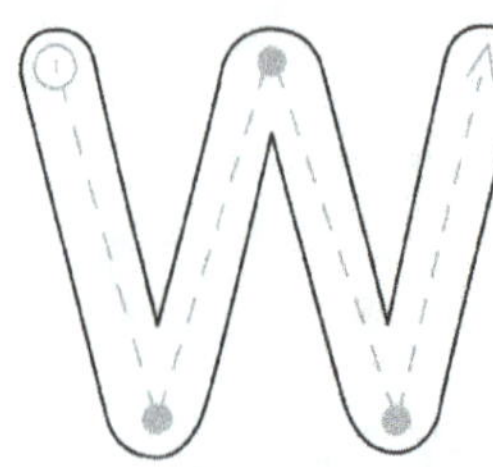

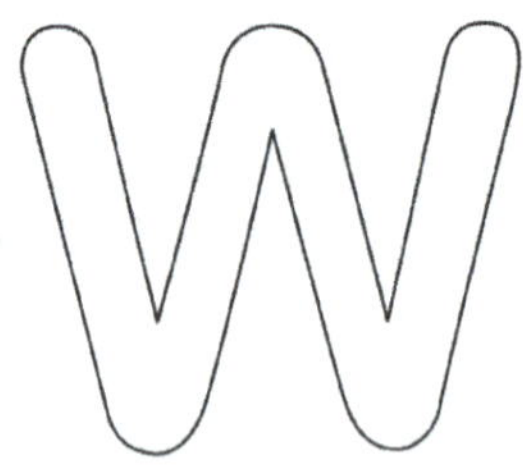

Watermelon **Worm**

Whale

ENGLISH
SPANISH
Watermelon
Sandía
Watermelon
Sandía
Whale
Ballena
Whale
Ballena
Worm
Gusano
Worm
Gusano

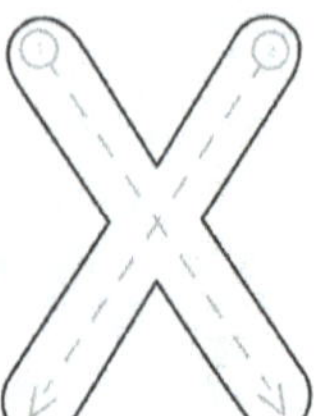
Xenops

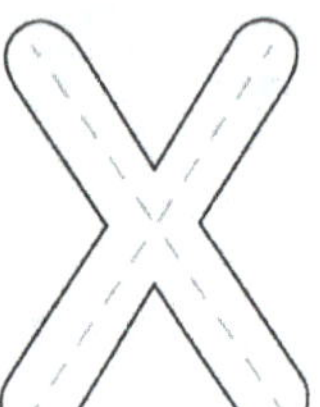
X-ray

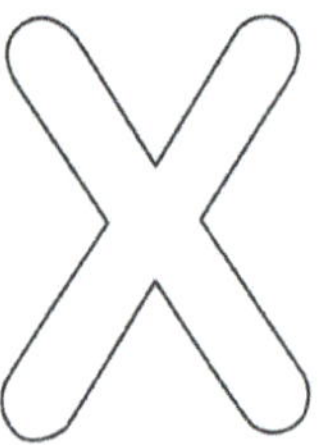
Xylophone

Xenops

X-ray

Xylophone

ENGLISH	SPANISH
Xenops	Xenops
Xylophone	Xilófono
X-ray	radiografía

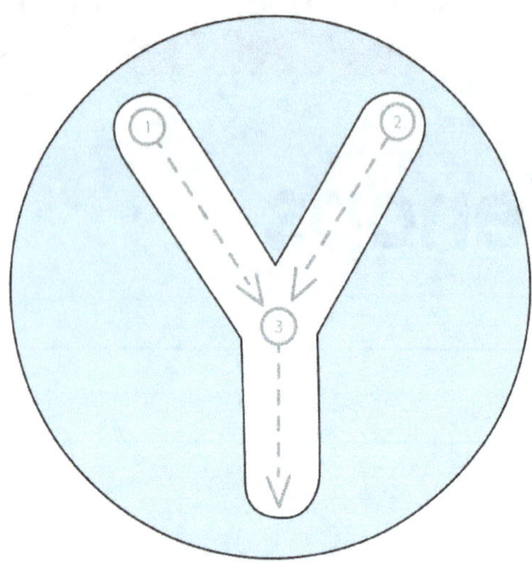

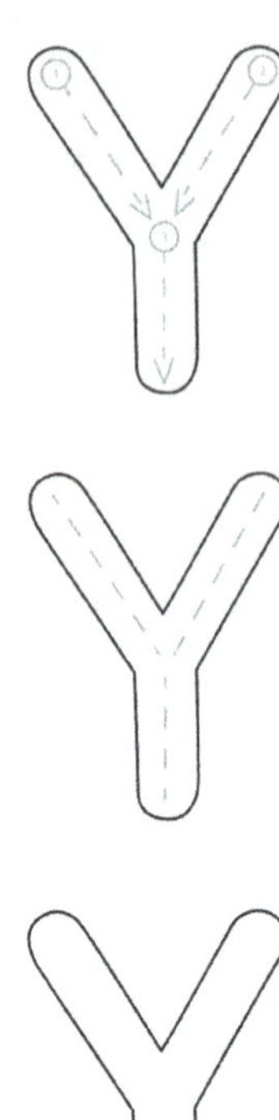

Yogurt

Yacht

Yarn

English	Spanish
Yogurt	**Yogur**
Yarn	**Hilo**
Yacht	**Yate**

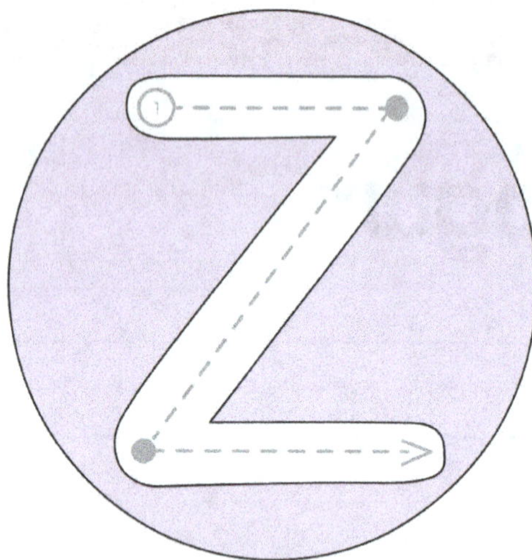

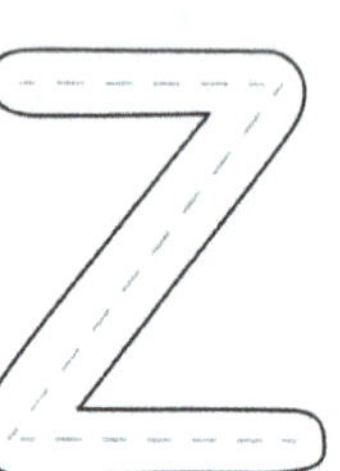

Zebra

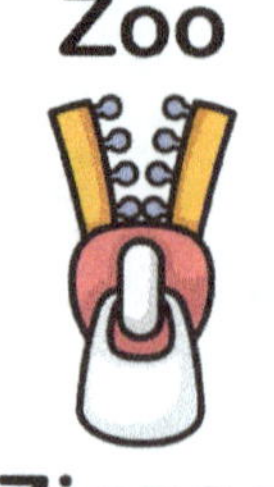
Zoo

Zipper

Zebra

Zoo

Zipper

<table>
<tr><td></td><td></td></tr>
</table>

ENGLISH	SPANISH
Zebra	**Cebra**
Zebra	Cebra
Zipper	**Cremallera**
Zipper	Cremallera
Zoo	**Zoo**
Zoo	Zoo

1. Cap

2. Grapes

3. Sheep

4. Ladybug

5. Flower

6. House

ANSWERS

Write the spanish word of the following:

	English	Spanish
1.	Cap	Gorra
2.	Grapes	Uva
3.	Sheep	Oveja
4.	Ladybug	Mariquita
5.	Flower	Flor
6.	House	Casa

Visit

BABY PROFESSOR
EDUCATION KIDS

www.BabyProfessorBooks.com
to download Free Baby Professor eBooks
and view our catalog of new and exciting
Children's Books